School RULES!

MATH

shortcuts, secrets, puzzles, and tricks to help you become a math master

by Emma MacLaren Henke
illustrated by Rebecca Jones

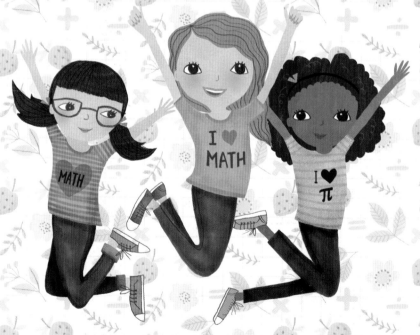

★ American Girl®

Published by American Girl Publishing

16 17 18 19 20 21 22 23 LEO 10 9 8 7 6 5 4 3 2 1

Editorial Development: Darcie Johnston
Art Direction & Design: Sarah Jane Boecher
Production: Jeannette Bailey, Virginia Gunderson, Mary Makarushka, Cynthia Stiles
Illustrations: Rebecca Jones
Special thanks to Tanya Zempel

Library of Congress Cataloging-in-Publication Data
Henke, Emma MacLaren, author.
School rules! Math : shortcuts, secrets, puzzles, and tricks to help you become a
math master / by Emma MacLaren Henke ; illustrated by Rebecca Jones.
pages   cm
ISBN 978-1-60958-744-4 (pbk.) — ISBN 978-1-60958-763-5 (ebook)
1. Mathematics—Study and teaching (Elementary)—Juvenile literature.
2. Arithmetic—Juvenile literature. I. Jones, Rebecca, illustrator. II. Title.
QA135.6.H46 2016   513—dc23   2015025308

americangirl.com/service

Dear Reader,

Why does math matter? Because we all use math every day! Think how often you wonder . . .

"How much?"

"How many?"

"How far?"

"When?"

Without math, you couldn't answer any of these questions.

Math lights up your brain differently than some other subjects do. Learning math can even feel sort of like learning a foreign language. It puzzles you and prompts you to think in new ways. And all it takes to get good at math is practice!

So sharpen your pencils and read on. The advice, tricks, games, and exercises in this book will help build the confidence you need to make the most of your mathematical mind.

Your friends at American Girl

contents

countdown!

BUILDING BLOCKS

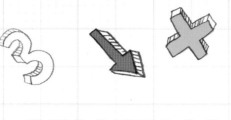

practice makes progress

MATH IN REAL LIFE

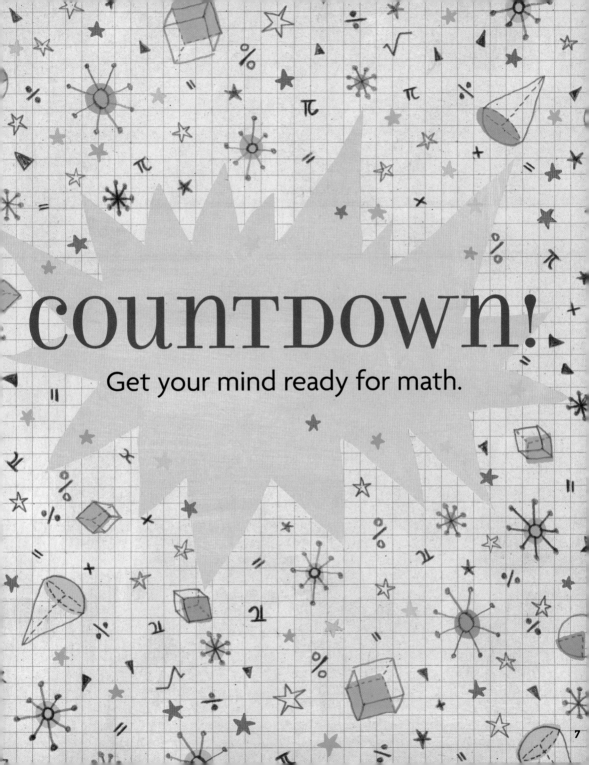

countdown!

Get your mind ready for math.

are you mad for math?

When you think about math, does your brain rev up or shut down?

1. All day long, I find myself counting, figuring time, and wondering, *How long? How far? How many?*

Sounds like me.
That's not me.

2. I'll often choose to do my math homework first.

Sounds like me.
That's not me.

3. Sometimes I worry that math is a subject I'll never be good at.

Sounds like me.
That's not me.

4. Math tests make me nervous.

Sounds like me.
That's not me.

5. I'd feel comfortable tutoring a friend who's having a hard time in math class.

Sounds like me.
That's not me.

8. When I get stuck on a challenging math problem, I give up trying to solve it pretty quickly.

Sounds like me.
That's not me.

9. My friends think I'm a math whiz!

Sounds like me.
That's not me.

Sounds like me.
That's not me.

7. I can picture myself working in a job where I'll need great math skills, such as teacher, banker, computer scientist, or accountant.

Sounds like me.
That's not me.

6. I wonder why we have to study so much math in school. We have calculators and computers, right?

Answers

Did you choose mostly **violet** answers? If so, you have a super-positive math-titude! You like the way it feels when math challenges you, and you enjoy using your mind in a mathematical way. This book is for you because it will show you new ways to think about math and new tricks to explore the subject you love.

Did you pick **blue** answers the most? You might feel a bit uncomfortable with math. That's OK! This book is for you because it can help you understand how you do math all the time, every day, without even thinking about it. Plus, you'll discover cool tools to boost your math confidence and strategies to help you understand math better than you ever thought you could.

Whether math is your favorite subject or your favorite subject to avoid, your brain is made for math. Every time you take a step, your mind figures how far to move your foot. Every time you catch a ball, your mind calculates how fast it's coming toward you and tells you when to put up your hands. In math class, you learn the concepts behind things your body and mind do naturally.

TOOLS OF THE TRADE

Prep for success with the right supplies.

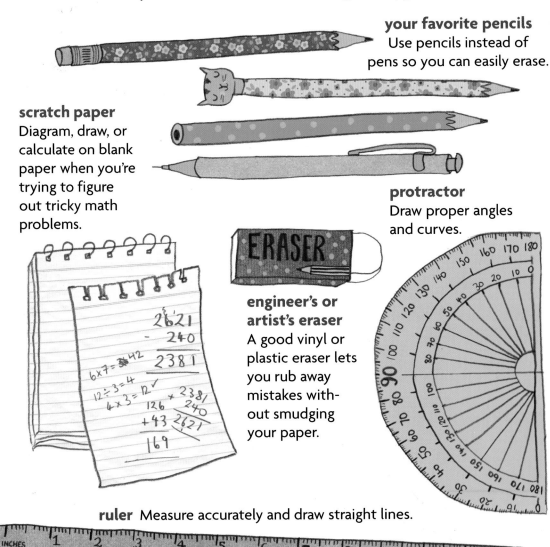

your favorite pencils
Use pencils instead of pens so you can easily erase.

scratch paper
Diagram, draw, or calculate on blank paper when you're trying to figure out tricky math problems.

protractor
Draw proper angles and curves.

engineer's or artist's eraser
A good vinyl or plastic eraser lets you rub away mistakes without smudging your paper.

ruler Measure accurately and draw straight lines.

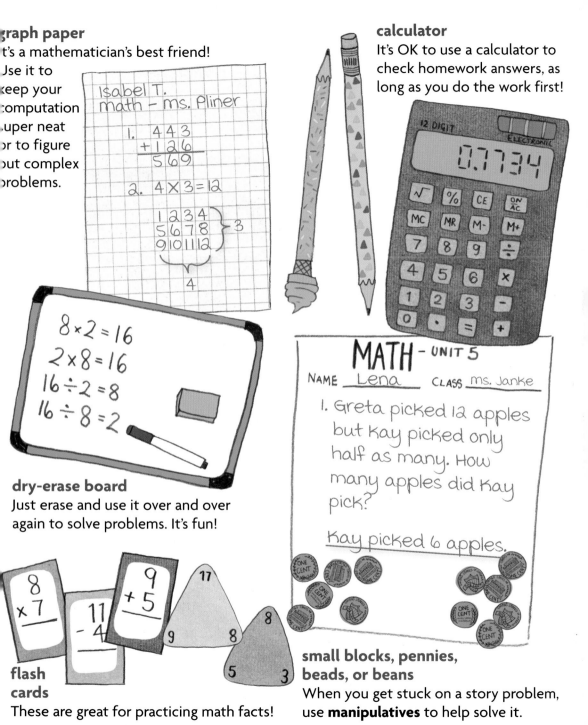

graph paper

It's a mathematician's best friend! Use it to keep your computation super neat or to figure out complex problems.

Isabel T.
math – ms. Pliner

1. 443
   +126
   ‾‾‾‾‾
    569

2. 4 × 3 = 12

1 2 3 4
5 6 7 8 } 3
9 10 11 12

4

calculator

It's OK to use a calculator to check homework answers, as long as you do the work first!

12 DIGIT
ELECTRONIC
0.7734

√   %   CE   ON/AC
MC MR M-   M+
7   8   9   ÷
4   5   6   ×
1   2   3   −
0   •   =   +

dry-erase board

Just erase and use it over and over again to solve problems. It's fun!

8 × 2 = 16
2 × 8 = 16
16 ÷ 2 = 8
16 ÷ 8 = 2

MATH – UNIT 5

NAME __Lena__   CLASS __ms. Janke__

1. Greta picked 12 apples but Kay picked only half as many. How many apples did Kay pick?

__Kay picked 6 apples.__

flash cards

These are great for practicing math facts!

8
× 7
‾‾‾

9
+ 5
‾‾‾

11
− 4
‾‾‾

17

8

8

5   3

small blocks, pennies, beads, or beans

When you get stuck on a story problem, use **manipulatives** to help solve it.

Terrific Triangles

When you need to memorize math facts, triangle-shaped flash cards can point you in the right direction.

Triangle flash cards help you master **fact families.** With these cards, you do more than just memorize math facts. You also see how addition is related to subtraction and how multiplication is related to division.

A single set of cards is used for both addition and subtraction. One point of a card shows a **sum** (the total, or the answer to an addition problem), and the other two points show the **addends**—the numbers that add up to the sum.

Here's how each card works.

ADDITION

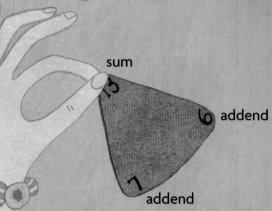

Quiz yourself by covering the sum with your thumb. Look at the two addends, and think out or call out the sum.

$$7 + 6 = 13 \qquad 6 + 7 = 13$$

SUBTRACTION

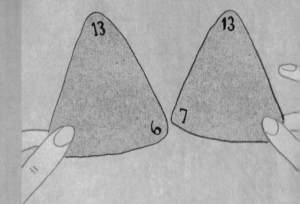

Quiz yourself by covering one addend. Look at the sum, and subtract the addend that's not covered to figure out the addend that's hidden. Then cover the other addend and do it again.

$$13 - 6 = 7 \qquad 13 - 7 = 6$$

Another card set is used for both multiplication and division. One point of each card shows a **product** (the answer to a multiplication problem). The other two points show **factors**—the numbers you multiply together to get the product.

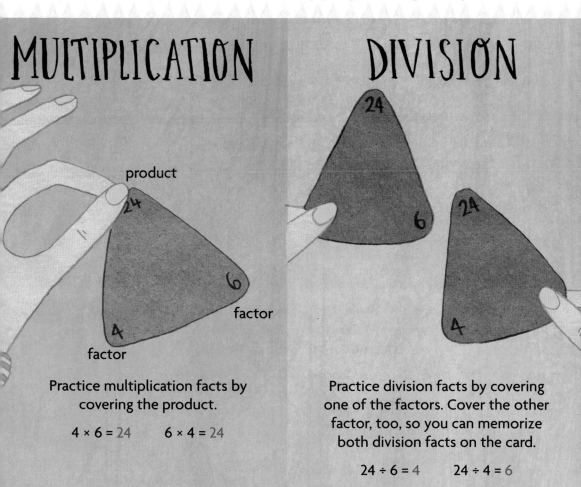

MULTIPLICATION

product

factor

factor

Practice multiplication facts by covering the product.

4 × 6 = 24   6 × 4 = 24

DIVISION

Practice division facts by covering one of the factors. Cover the other factor, too, so you can memorize both division facts on the card.

24 ÷ 6 = 4   24 ÷ 4 = 6

In math, paying attention to patterns pays off. Triangle flash cards help you learn addends and sums, and factors and products, as groups of numbers that go together. Thinking about math facts in these groups will take you farther than just memorizing math answers. When you make sense of numbers this way, it can make learning math so much easier!

Clever Calculator

Use your calculator to perform math magic!

Favorite Number

1. Tell a friend to name her favorite number from 1 to 9.

2. Give your friend your calculator, and instruct her to multiply the number she picked by 9.

3. Then tell her to multiply the result by 12,345,679 (the numbers 1 through 9 in order, without the 8).

4. Ask her to show you the calculator.

You both will see a 9-digit number in which every digit is the number your friend selected. If she chose 3, for example, the calculator will show 333333333.

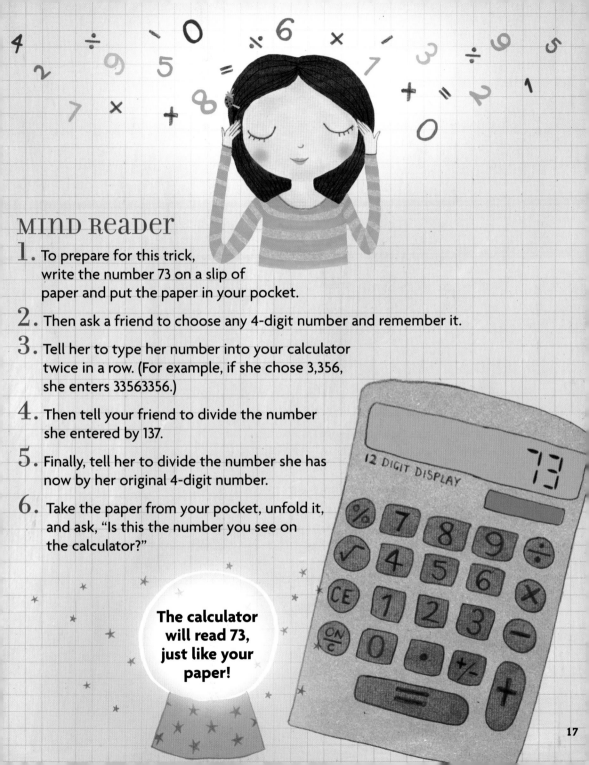

MIND READER

1. To prepare for this trick, write the number 73 on a slip of paper and put the paper in your pocket.

2. Then ask a friend to choose any 4-digit number and remember it.

3. Tell her to type her number into your calculator twice in a row. (For example, if she chose 3,356, she enters 33563356.)

4. Then tell your friend to divide the number she entered by 137.

5. Finally, tell her to divide the number she has now by her original 4-digit number.

6. Take the paper from your pocket, unfold it, and ask, "Is this the number you see on the calculator?"

The calculator will read 73, just like your paper!

THE STORY OF MATH

Math teachers always say, "Show your work!"
Here's what makes it so important.

You have a story in mind. It's a wonderful, funny, interesting story. And you decide to tell it. So you write,

She lived happily ever after. The end.

That's not much of a story, is it?

Math problems are like stories. The work you use to figure out the answer to a problem is as important as all the twists and turns of a good tale. When you do math, you want to get the correct solution, but it's usually more important to be able to explain *how* you got it. You have to tell the whole story!

> Elsa and Sabrina ride the school bus. Elsa lives 3 miles from school, and Sabrina lives 5 miles from school. If the bus takes each girl directly from home to school and back again, how many more miles does Sabrina ride the bus each day than Elsa?

This particular problem is not that complex. Perhaps you see quickly that the solution is 4 miles. But "4 miles" is not the complete story, is it?

SCHOOL BUS

Elsa and Sabrina ride the school bus. Elsa lives 3 miles from school, and Sabrina lives 5 miles from school. If the bus takes each girl directly from home to school and back again, how many more miles does Sabrina ride the bus each day than Elsa?

Sabrina

5 miles   5 miles $5+5=10$

Elsa

3 miles   3 miles $3+3=6$

$10-6=4$ Sabrina rides the bus 4 miles more than Elsa each day.

THAT'S the whole story!

Drawing pictures helps you figure out problems that don't seem simple. In the story of Elsa and Sabrina and the school bus, when you draw how far each girl travels each day, it's easy to see the difference.

Get in the habit of always showing your work, even when a problem seems easy. That way, when problems get harder, you'll be used to showing your work and drawing pictures to solve them. This will make math much easier as you get older!

OK, now let's try a basic multiplication problem.

54 × 78 = ?

54 × 78 = 4,212

Yes, true enough, the solution is 4,212. But it's best to show how you found your solution.

54 × 78 = ?

Showing your work proves to you and your teacher that you understand what you're learning. And if you're having trouble, your work will show what part you don't understand so that you can get help and stop making the same error. You'll be telling the whole story!

teacher test

Think your math teacher expects you to earn 100% every time? Take this quiz to discover what your teacher *really* wants.

1 Racing through your math work to be the first student to turn in every assignment is a great way to show off your smarts.

True or False

2 Math teachers think your homework should be perfect every time. You had all night to get it right!

True or False

3 Math teachers insist there's only one correct way to solve every math problem.

True or False

4 Math teachers feel you should volunteer to answer a question in class or show work at the board only if you're absolutely sure you'll get it right.

True or False

5 Math teachers hate it when students ask questions in class. If you don't understand something, figure it out on your own!

True or False

6 Math teachers expect you to earn an A on every test and quiz.

True or False

answers

1 False! Teachers know that students work at different speeds. Teachers want you to do careful work and to try to do your best. If there's time, they hope you check your answers.

2 False! Teachers expect students to make mistakes on math homework. Math homework lets you practice the concepts you cover in class. Teachers look at homework to see if you understand what they're teaching. If students don't do well on a particular homework assignment, a teacher knows to spend more time explaining that topic.

3 False! Teachers know brains work in different ways and there's more than one way to arrive at an answer. They love it when students find new ways to solve math problems. So share your solutions if you have the chance. Maybe your idea will help another student understand the problem.

4 False! Teachers want to know how well all their students understand math material, not just the math whizzes and the kids who already know how to do it. They know kids don't usually understand something the first time they learn it. It takes a few times to fully understand a concept—especially with math!

5 False! Math teachers may be disappointed if you raise your hand and say, "I don't get it" without giving yourself time to understand the problem. But it's great to ask questions in class. It shows you're trying, and teachers want to know what their students need help with. Also, other students probably have the same question and they're happy you asked.

6 False! Teachers expect you to prepare for tests and to do careful work. They expect you to talk to them well before the test if you're having a hard time understanding the material. But they don't expect you to ace every exam. Just do your best.

Whether you're a math whiz or someone who struggles with the subject, teachers are looking for progress and effort, not for perfection. They want your understanding of math to grow. Making mistakes is one of the best ways to learn!

Making Mistakes HELPS YOU Learn!

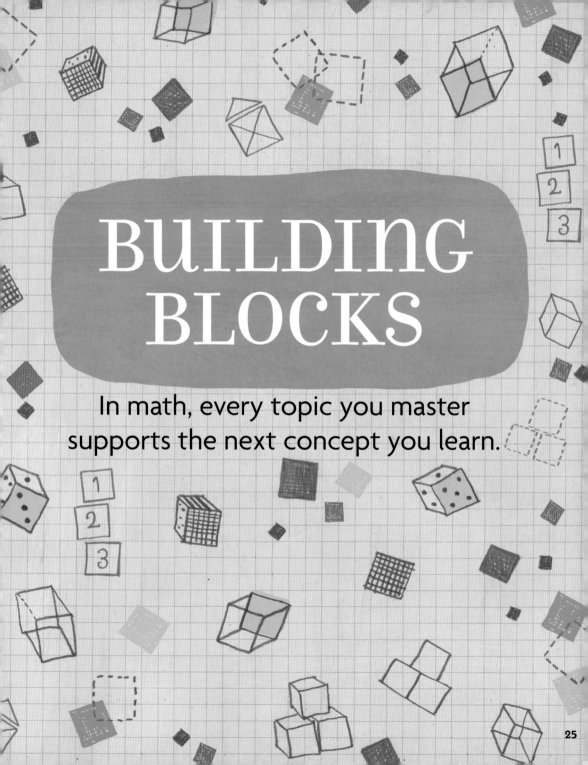

BUILDING BLOCKS

In math, every topic you master supports the next concept you learn.

NIFTY NUMBERS

Going back to basics helps you see number patterns
in your most challenging math work.

GREATER THAN & LESS THAN

Did you ever notice that young kids usually learn to count before they can read
or write? When Mom serves cookies, kids know 2 cookies is more than 1. When
Dad reads bedtime stories, 3 books last longer than 2 books. We all come with
a built-in sense of **greater than.**

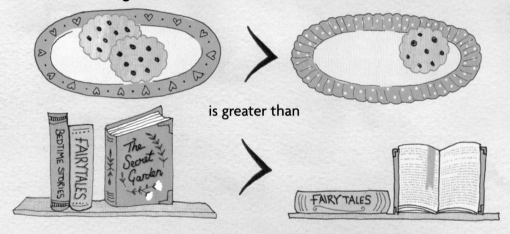

is greater than

And of course, we have a similar understanding of **less than.**

is less than

How can you remember these symbols? The bigger end of the sign is next
to the bigger number. And the small, pointy end points to the smaller number.

WHOLE NUMBERS, FRACTIONS & DECIMALS

As you probably know, young math students also learn to think of numbers along a line.

For example, a simple problem looks like this: **7 + 3 = ?**

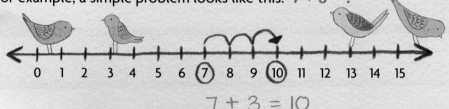

$$7 + 3 = 10$$

The number line can help you see the solution to more complex problems, too.

Celine brought 15 lollipops to school. She gave out 5 lollipops to her friends on the bus, 6 lollipops to her friends at lunch, and 2 lollipops to her locker partners. How many lollipops did Celine have left?

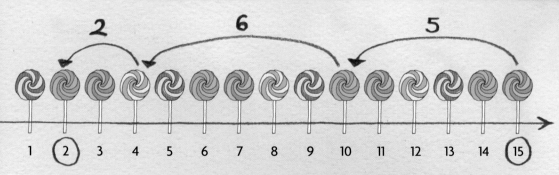

Celine had 2 lollipops left.

Numbers get higher to the right and lower to the left. In both directions, numbers keep on going through **infinity.** That means the numbers continue, without ending.

The number line also shows space between the numbers. That's because each individual **whole number** ("counting numbers" such as 1, 2, 3, 4, and so on) can be broken down into an infinite number of smaller parts, such as halves or sixteenths or millionths.

In the language of math, these smaller parts of numbers can be shown as

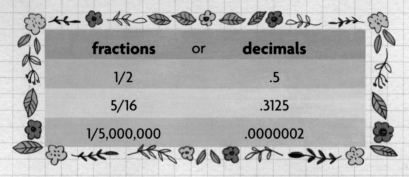

fractions	or	decimals
1/2		.5
5/16		.3125
1/5,000,000		.0000002

So, for example: $1 = 1/2 + 1/2$ is the same as $1 = .5 + .5$

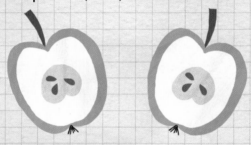

And $1 = 1/4 + 1/4 + 1/4 + 1/4$ is the same as $1 = .25 + .25 + .25 + .25$

The number line is a good example of how pictures help you understand math ideas. The next time you get stuck, try drawing a picture to help yourself see the solution.

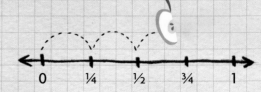

0   ¼   ½   ¾   1

EVENS & ODDS

Whole numbers are either **even** or **odd.**
Even numbers are numbers that can be divided by 2.

2, 4, 6, 8, 10, 12, 14, 16, 18, 20, 22...

$$4 \div 2 = 2$$

$$36 \div 2 = 18$$

$$250 \div 2 = 125$$

Odd numbers are not divisible by 2.
That is, they cannot be divided into two equal, whole-number parts.

1, 3, 5, 7, 9, 11, 13, 15, 17, 19, 21, 23, 25...

$$5 \div 2 = 2\frac{1}{2}$$

$$45 \div 2 = 22\frac{1}{2}$$

$$201 \div 2 = 100\frac{1}{2}$$

Base 10

Numbers are made up of **digits,** the same way that words are made of letters. In our number system, called **Base 10,** we use single digits for the numbers 0 through 9. We don't have a single digit for the number 10—or any number higher than 10. The two-digit number 10 stands for 1 ten and 0 ones. The three-digit number 100 stands for 1 hundred, 0 tens, and 0 ones. Each digit is in a place that's ten times bigger than the place to its right. This Base 10 system helps us understand **place value.** To know the value of a digit, you just look at its place.

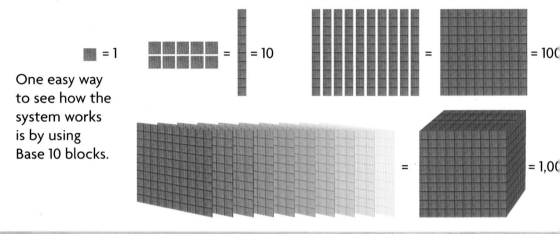

One easy way to see how the system works is by using Base 10 blocks.

$\blacksquare = 1$ $\quad = \quad = 10$ $\quad = 100$

$= 1,00$

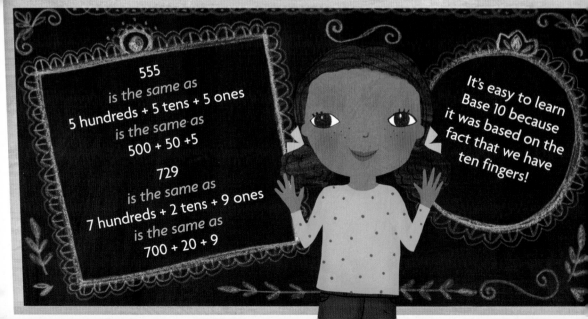

555
is the same as
5 hundreds + 5 tens + 5 ones
is the same as
500 + 50 + 5

729
is the same as
7 hundreds + 2 tens + 9 ones
is the same as
700 + 20 + 9

It's easy to learn Base 10 because it was based on the fact that we have ten fingers!

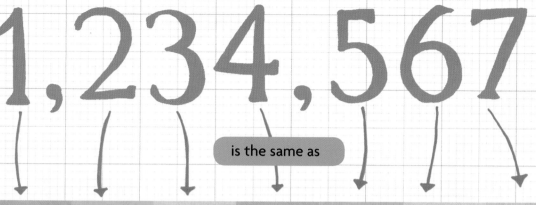

1,234,567

is the same as

1,000,000	100,000	10,000	1,000	100	10	1
Millions place	Hundred thousands place	Ten thousands place	Thousands place	Hundreds place	Tens place	Ones place
1,	2	3	4,	5	6	7

is the same as

1 million + 2 hundred thousands + 3 ten thousands + 4 thousands + 5 hundreds + 6 tens + 7 ones

is the same as

1,000,000 + 200,000 + 30,000 + 4,000 + 500 + 60 + 7

After every three digits we stick in a comma, because that helps our brains understand the number more quickly without having to count out the places.

Quick—say this number out loud:

9236471

Not so easy, right?

Now say it:
9,236,471

BINGO BONANZA

Practice place value by playing bingo with your friends!

HOW TO PLAY

1. Before the game starts, make copies of the blank bingo card on page 34.

2. Each player gets her own blank card. (Multiply the fun by playing with more than one card!)

3. Players fill in their blank cards with a five-digit number in each of the five rows. Players can choose any numbers they like, and a number can have more than one of the same digit. For example, 12,121 and 98,752 are both fine. When the card is filled in, each square will contain one digit.

4. Choose one player to be the caller.

5. The caller writes a list of at least 30 five-digit numbers, then calls them out, in order, one at a time.

6. Using pennies or beans, players mark digits that match the number and place value of each number called out. For example, if the caller says the number 12,321, players can mark any 1 in their Ten Thousands column if they have one, any 2 in their Thousands column, any 3 in their Hundreds column, and so on.

7. A player can mark only one digit in a column for each number called. For example, if a player's card has two five-digit numbers that both have a 3 in the Hundreds place, and the called number is 12,345, the player can put a marker on only one of the 3s on this play.

8. The first player to mark a vertical, horizontal, or diagonal line across her card shouts "Bingo!" and wins the round. Check the winning card against the caller's list of numbers.

9. Choose a new caller for each round.

10. To make rounds last longer, play until someone fills her entire card.

BINGO BONANZA

Ten Thousands	Thousands	Hundreds	Tens	Ones

pluses & minuses

Mastering these two operations makes a difference in the sum of your math know-how!

ADDITION

Addition is the math operation you use to find the **sum** (total) of **addends** (numbers put together). With your triangle flash cards, memorize addition facts for numbers from 0 to 10. Memorizing is a must—all the other math operations build on addition!

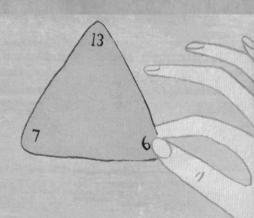

SUBTRACTION

Subtraction and addition work together. They are called **inverse operations** of each other. With addition, the solution is the sum of numbers. With subtraction, the solution is the **difference** between numbers. Another way to look at subtraction is that you're finding a missing addend instead of a sum.

Once you learn to read, you don't have to keep sounding out every word. You recognize many words by sight, so you can focus on learning new words and the ideas in the sentences. It's the same with memorizing your pluses and minuses. When you know math facts by sight, doing math—and learning new math concepts—becomes so much easier. Triangle flash cards help you know fact families by sight and understand how addition and subtraction work together.

SUBTRACTING LARGE NUMBERS

When you're subtracting large numbers, remember this rhyme:

More on top?
No need to stop.

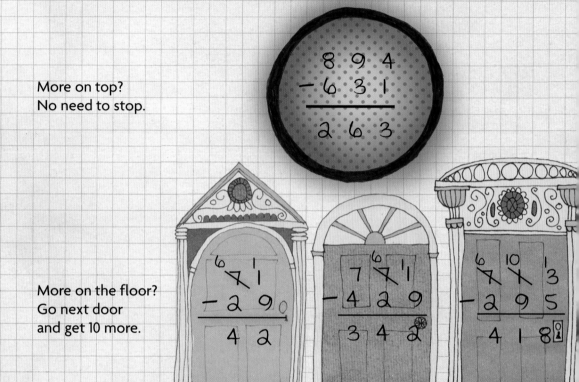

```
  8 9 4
- 6 3 1
-------
  2 6 3
```

More on the floor?
Go next door
and get 10 more.

```
  ⁶7̶ ¹1
- 2 9 0̶
-------
    4 2
```

```
  7 ⁶7̶ ¹1
- 4 2 9
-------
  3 4 2̶
```

```
  ⁶7̶ ¹⁰0̶ 1
- 2 9 5
-------
  4 1 8
```

Number's the same?
Zero's the game.

```
  4 6 4
- 2 6 4
-------
  2 0 0
```

NUMBER FUN

PUZZLE PALOOZA!

Familiar word games do double duty as number puzzles.

CRISS-CROSS MATH

Solve the sums (+) and differences (−) to fill in this math-tastic crossword. Use numbers for your answers— no letters or words.

(answer on page 92)

(answer on page 92)

ACROSS

1. 9,999 − 3,131 = ?

4. 2,608 + 1,616 = ?

6. 999 − 12 = ?

8. 12,345 − 6,345 = ?

9. 10,000 − 4,999 = ?

12. 9,999 + 10,001 = ?

14. 1 + 2 + 3 + 4 + 5 + 6 + 7 + 8 + 9 + 10 = ?

15. 75.5 + 25.5 = ?

DOWN

2. 599 + 79 = ?

3. 55 − 11 = ?

5. 12,335 + 12,345 = ?

6. 500 + 400 = ?

7. 777,777 + 232,324 = ?

9. 499 + 44 = ?

10. 20,000 − 7,655 = ?

11. 6,029 − 5,000 = ?

13. 31 + 50 = ?

sum search

Look for strings of numbers that have a sum of exactly 100. Sum strings will contain two or more numbers, and they can be horizontal, vertical, or diagonal, just like in a word search. There are at least 10 strings of numbers that add up to 100 in the puzzle. Happy adding!

40	30	20	10	17	16	4
5	9	42	80	9	33	5
50	12	39	10	33	14	18
5	50	99	33	21	18	19
88	24	1	94	19	25	5
33	35	38	20	19	25	1
54	29	21	44	21	25	7
14	22	10	15	20	25	30

(answer on page 92)

THE BEST OF TIMES

Memorize multiplication facts using tables, tricks, and triangle flash cards.

In multiplication, your job is to find the total when you add a number to itself a certain number of times. Remember: The numbers you multiply together are called **factors,** and the solution is called the **product.**

1.
$$\begin{array}{r} 5 \\ \times\ 3 \\ \hline 15 \end{array}$$

→ *is the same as* →

2. $5 + 5 + 5 = 15$

↓

is the same as

↙

3.

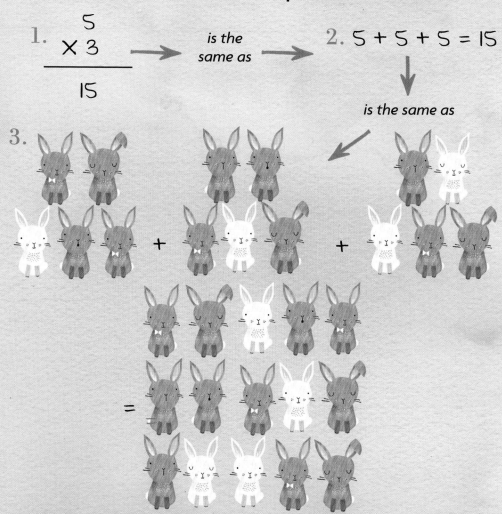

rimes Table

ll the products for factors from 1 to 10!

×	1	2	3	4	5	6	7	8	9	10
1	1	2	3	4	5	6	7	8	9	10
2	2	4	6	8	10	12	14	16	18	20
3	3	6	9	12	15	18	21	24	27	30
4	4	8	12	16	20	24	28	32	36	40
5	5	10	15	20	25	30	35	40	45	50
6	6	12	18	24	30	36	42	48	54	60
7	7	14	21	28	35	42	49	56	63	70
8	8	16	24	32	40	48	56	64	72	80
9	9	18	27	36	45	54	63	72	81	90
10	10	20	30	40	50	60	70	80	90	100

TIMES TABLE TACTICS

Figure products fast with these clever tricks.

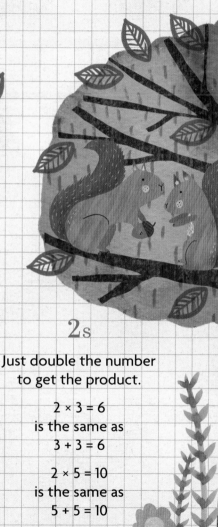

1s

Any number
times 1 is itself.

$1 \times 1 = 1$

$1 \times 2 = 2$

$1 \times 5 = 5$

$1 \times 100 = 100$

2s

Just double the number
to get the product.

$2 \times 3 = 6$
is the same as
$3 + 3 = 6$

$2 \times 5 = 10$
is the same as
$5 + 5 = 10$

$2 \times 8 = 16$
is the same as
$8 + 8 = 16$

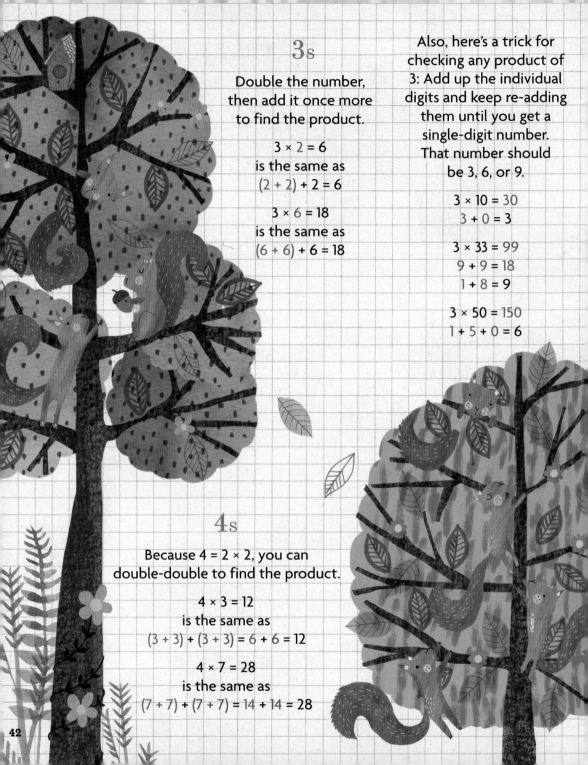

3s

Double the number,
then add it once more
to find the product.

$3 \times 2 = 6$
is the same as
$(2 + 2) + 2 = 6$

$3 \times 6 = 18$
is the same as
$(6 + 6) + 6 = 18$

Also, here's a trick for
checking any product of
3: Add up the individual
digits and keep re-adding
them until you get a
single-digit number.
That number should
be 3, 6, or 9.

$3 \times 10 = 30$
$3 + 0 = 3$

$3 \times 33 = 99$
$9 + 9 = 18$
$1 + 8 = 9$

$3 \times 50 = 150$
$1 + 5 + 0 = 6$

4s

Because $4 = 2 \times 2$, you can
double-double to find the product.

$4 \times 3 = 12$
is the same as
$(3 + 3) + (3 + 3) = 6 + 6 = 12$

$4 \times 7 = 28$
is the same as
$(7 + 7) + (7 + 7) = 14 + 14 = 28$

42

5s

If you multiply an even number by 5, the product will end in 0. If you multiply an odd number by 5, the product will end in 5.

$5 \times 2 = 10$

$5 \times 4 = 20$

$5 \times 8 = 40$

and

$5 \times 1 = 5$

$5 \times 3 = 15$

$5 \times 7 = 35$

6s

When you multiply an even number by 6, the last digit of the product will be the same as the last digit of the even number.

$6 \times 2 = 12$

$6 \times 16 = 96$

$6 \times 438 = 2,628$

7s

Try counting by 7s to arrive at your product.

$7 \times 7 = 49$

7
14
21
28
35
42
49

8s

Double-up the 4s times tables.

$8 \times 3 = 24$
is the same as
$(4 \times 3) + (4 \times 3) = 24$
is the same as
$12 + 12 = 24$

43

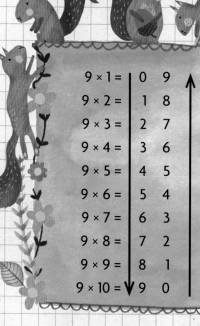

9s

Learn the products with these neat 9s patterns:

9 × 1 =	0	9
9 × 2 =	1	8
9 × 3 =	2	7
9 × 4 =	3	6
9 × 5 =	4	5
9 × 6 =	5	4
9 × 7 =	6	3
9 × 8 =	7	2
9 × 9 =	8	1
9 × 10 =	9	0

AND

9 × 1 = 9	9 = 9
9 × 2 = 18	1 + 8 = 9
9 × 3 = 27	2 + 7 = 9
9 × 4 = 36	3 + 6 = 9
9 × 5 = 45	4 + 5 = 9
9 × 6 = 54	5 + 4 = 9
9 × 7 = 63	6 + 3 = 9
9 × 8 = 72	7 + 2 = 9
9 × 9 = 81	8 + 1 = 9
9 × 10 = 90	9 + 0 = 9

Or, use your very own finger calculator! Just hold your hands in front of you with your palms facing down. Starting on the left (with your left pinkie), count out the factor that is not the 9. Bend down the finger you land on. The bent finger will separate the tens from the ones. That is, the number of fingers to the left of your bent finger will be the number in the tens place of your product, and the number of fingers to the right will be the number in the ones place.

Give it a try! For example, to multiply 9 × 3 (or 3 × 9), count three fingers on your left hand and bend the third—the middle finger. That gives you two fingers in the tens place and seven fingers in the ones place:

9 × 3 = 27!

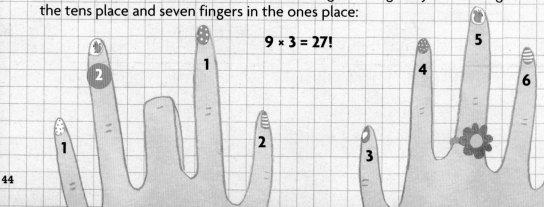

10s

Just add a zero to the other factor to find your product!

$10 \times 1 = 10$

$10 \times 2 = 20$

$10 \times 3 = 30$

$10 \times 4 = 40$

$10 \times 5 = 50$

$10 \times 6 = 60$

$10 \times 7 = 70$

$10 \times 8 = 80$

$10 \times 9 = 90$

$10 \times 10 = 100$

squares

A number squared is that number multiplied by itself.
They are called squares because they always make a square.

$1 \times 1 = 1$

$2 \times 2 = 4$

$3 \times 3 = 9$

DIVIDE & CONQUER

Division and multiplication are like two sides of the same coin.

You use division to separate a number into equal parts. The number you separate, or divide, is called the **dividend.** The number of groups you separate the dividend into is the **divisor.** And the resulting number in each group is the **quotient.**

| 15 is the dividend | → | $15 \div 5 = 3$ | ← | 3 is the quotient |

5 is the divisor

You can also write this division problem as: $5\overline{)15}$ with quotient 3

Or you can think of it by drawing something like this:

46

Like addition and subtraction, multiplication and division are inverse operations of each other. Since they are related, they are fact families. If you know your multiplication facts, you know division facts, too. In division, you're given one multiplication factor and the product, and you have to figure out the other factor. Your triangle flash cards can help you see this.

With this card:
24 ÷ 4 = ?
and
4 × ? = 24
(? = 6)

With this card:
90 ÷ 9 = ?
and
9 × ? = 90
(? = 10)

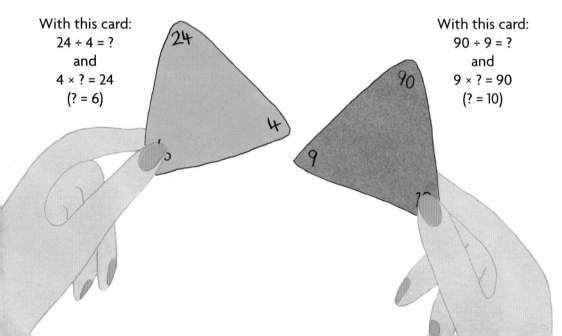

IS IT DIVISIBLE?

Try these **divisibility rules** to see if a number is evenly divisible by the numbers 2 through 10. (When a number is evenly divisible, there's no **remainder** left over.)

2

All even numbers—that is, all numbers that end in 0, 2, 4, 6, or 8—are divisible by 2.

3

Add up the digits in the number. If the sum of the digits is divisible by 3, the number is divisible by 3. 432 ... 4+3+2=9 ... is 9 divisible by 3? YES

4

If the last two digits of a number are divisible by 4, the number is divisible by 4. 612 ... is 12 divisible by 4? YES

5

If the number ends in 5 or 0, it is divisible by 5.

6

If the number is divisible by both 2 and 3, then it is also divisible by 6. 84 ... is it divisible by both 2 and 3? YES

7

Take the last digit of a number and double it. Subtract that number from the remaining digits. If the number left over is 0 or a positive or negative number divisible by 7, the starting number is divisible by 7. 28 ... 8+8=16 ... 2-16= -14 ... is -14 divisible by 7? YES Too complicated? Just divide by 7 and check!

8

If the last three digits of a number are divisible by 8, the number is divisible by 8. 23,456 ... is 456 divisible by 8? YES

9

If you add all the digits together and that sum is divisible by 9, the number is divisible by 9. 5,283 ... 5+2+8+3=18 ... is 18 divisible by 9? YES

10

If the number ends in 0, it is divisible by 10.

MATH MAZE

Follow the arrows with correct answers
to find your way from start to finish!

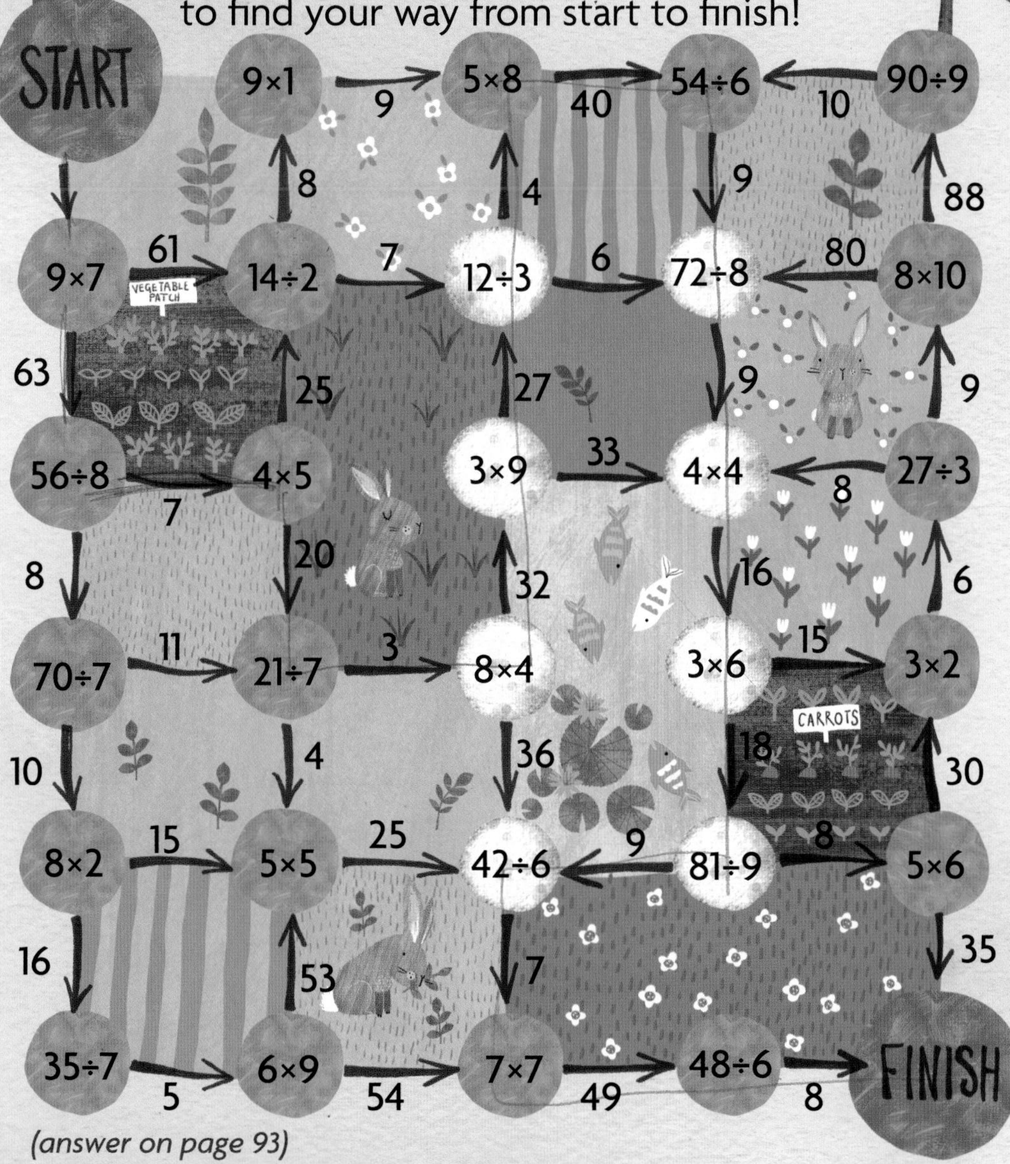

START

9×1 → 9 → 5×8 → 40 → 54÷6 ← 90÷9 ← 10

8 ↑   4 ↑   9 ↓   88 ↑

9×7   61 → 14÷2   7 → 12÷3   6 → 72÷8 ← 80 ← 8×10

63 ↓   25 ↓   27 ↑   9 ↓   9 ↑

56÷8 ← 4×5   3×9 → 33 → 4×4 ← 8 ← 27÷3
       7

8 ↓   20 ↓   32 ↓   16 ↓   6 ↑

70÷7   11 → 21÷7   3 → 8×4   3×6   15 → 3×2

10 ↓   4 ↓   36 ↓   18 ↓   30 ↓

8×2   15 → 5×5   25 → 42÷6 ← 9 ← 81÷9   8 → 5×6

16 ↓   53 ↑   7 ↓   35 ↓

35÷7 → 5 → 6×9 → 54 → 7×7 → 49 → 48÷6 → 8 → FINISH

VEGETABLE PATCH
CARROTS

(answer on page 93)

49

prime time

Roll your way down the path to learn prime numbers.

Prime numbers are positive whole numbers that are divisible by only 1 and themselves. So a prime number has just two factors: 1 and itself. Using these rules, it's easy to see that 2 is a prime number (the only even prime number!), followed by 3, 5, 7, and so on. The higher you count, the harder it is to find prime numbers.

Game Rules

For this game you need two or more players, a token for each player (such as a coin or paper clip), a six-sided die, and the game board on page 51.

1. Players take turns rolling the die and moving their token forward.

2. If a player lands on a prime number, she rolls again.

3. If a player claims she landed on a prime number but is proven wrong, she loses her next turn.

4. The first player who gets past 50 wins!

prime one?

1 does not count as a prime number because it's a factor of every number.

WELCOME TO BLUE LAKE PARK
START
1 2 3 4 5 6 7 8 9 10 11 12 13 14 15 16 17 18 19 20 21 22 23 24 25 26 27 28 29 30 31 32 33 34 35 36 37 38 39 40 41 42 43 44 45 46 47 48 49 50
BLUE LAKE
THE FOREST
FINISH
PICNIC SPOT

GOAL SCORE: 135.698

GOAL!

GOAL!

TEAM MATH

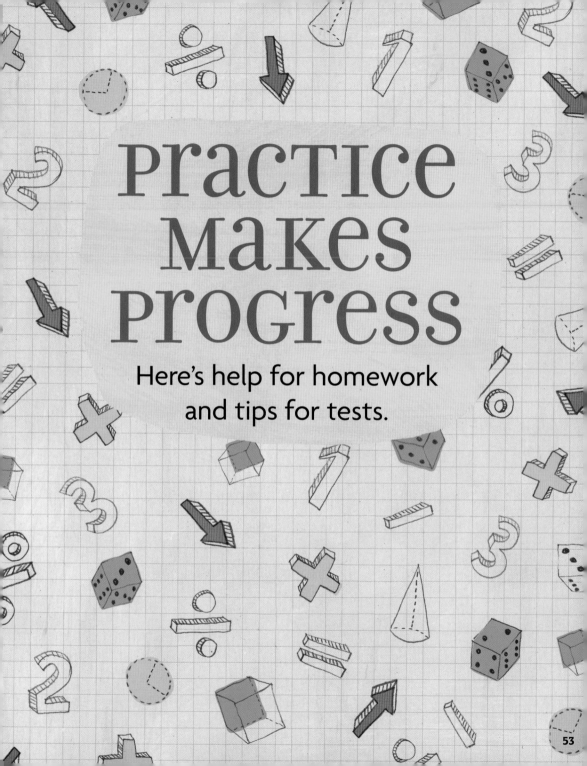

practice makes progress

Here's help for homework and tips for tests.

CHECK, PLEASE

Learn smart shortcuts for reviewing math work.

It's a good idea to check your math work before you turn it in. But you don't have to redo every problem. Try these techniques on your next assignment or test.

ROUNDING & ESTIMATES

Figure out roughly how much your solution should be to see if your answer is in the ballpark—in other words, close to what the answer should be.

For a problem like
$9,527 + 688 = 10,215$

think

$9,500 + 700 = 10,200$

If your solution was something much lower, like 1,025, or much higher, like 100,215, you'd know you made a mistake.

For a problem like
$3,127 \times 89 = 278,303$

think

$3,000 \times 100 = 300,000$

If your solution was something like 27,830 or 2,183,030, you'd know you made a mistake.

ODDS & EVENS

Paying attention to whether the numbers you're working with are odd or even can help you see if your solutions are correct. Follow these rules to check your answers when adding, subtracting, and multiplying. (The rules don't apply for division, since the answer might contain a fraction—and only whole numbers can be even or odd.)

Addition

even + even = even

odd + odd = even

even + odd = odd

odd + even = odd

Subtraction

even − even = even

odd − odd = even

even − odd = odd

odd − even = odd

Multiplication

even × even = even

odd × odd = odd

even × odd = even

odd × even = even

Negatives

If you're working with negative numbers, follow these rules:

Multiplication

negative × negative = positive

positive × positive = positive

negative × positive = negative

positive × negative = negative

Division

negative ÷ negative = positive

positive ÷ positive = positive

negative ÷ positive = negative

positive ÷ negative = negative

FLIP IT

Use the inverse operation to check your answer. Remember: Inverse means opposite. So addition and subtraction are inverse operations of each other, and multiplication and division are inverse operations of each other.

For addition problems like

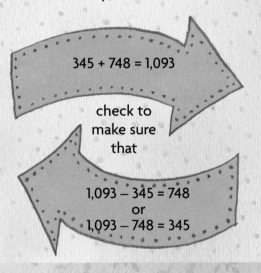

$345 + 748 = 1{,}093$

check to make sure that

$1{,}093 - 345 = 748$
or
$1{,}093 - 748 = 345$

For subtraction problems like

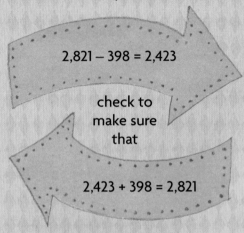

$2{,}821 - 398 = 2{,}423$

check to make sure that

$2{,}423 + 398 = 2{,}821$

For multiplication problems like

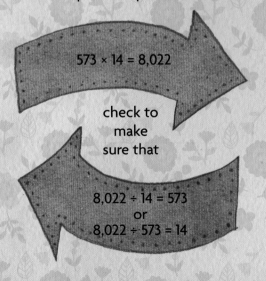

$573 \times 14 = 8{,}022$

check to make sure that

$8{,}022 \div 14 = 573$
or
$8{,}022 \div 573 = 14$

For division problems like

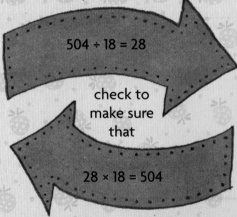

$504 \div 18 = 28$

check to make sure that

$28 \times 18 = 504$

CALCULATOR HELP

It's fine to use a calculator to check math homework, as long as you do the calculation on your own first. If you find an error, set the calculator aside and redo the problem.

WHY WORDS?

Answer some key questions, and you'll find
a happy ending to story problems.

Math story problems help you understand how math applies to real life. But sometimes students struggle to see the math problem inside the story. The next time you have trouble, just ask yourself these questions:

What am I trying to figure out?

What do I know already?

Take a look at this problem:

Grace and Gabby made cupcakes for the school bake sale. Grace sold 15 cupcakes for $2 each, and Gabby sold 12 cupcakes for $3 each. Altogether, how much money did the girls' cupcakes earn?

$2

$3

Grace and Gabby made cupcakes for the school bake sale. Grace sold 15 cupcakes for $2 each, and Gabby sold 12 cupcakes for $3 each. Altogether, how much money did the girls' cupcakes earn?

WHAT AM I TRYING TO FIGURE OUT?

Look for numbers and for key words like "how much," "how many," "how long," and "difference between" to spot what kind of solution you need. The last sentence in this problem ("Altogether, how much money did the girls' cupcakes earn?") tells you clearly what kind of solution the problem is looking for. The word "altogether" means addition, so your answer is going to be a dollar amount that is the total of all the money earned. Sometimes it helps to write the words for your solution before you do the math. You might pencil in:

> The cupcakes earned $____.

Just fill in the blank once you solve the math problem.

WHAT DO I KNOW ALREADY?

Make a list of all the information the story problem gives you. For this problem, you might write:

> Grace: 15 cupcakes for $2 each
> Gabby: 12 cupcakes for $3 each

You already know you're looking for the total money earned by both girls. So figure out how much each girl's cupcakes earned:

$$15 \times 2 = 30$$
$$12 \times 3 = 36$$

Then add those numbers together:

$$30 + 36 = 66$$

The girls' cupcakes earned $66.

Remember to draw pictures and diagrams to help yourself figure out story problems. Answer the key questions with your drawings to see the solutions!

Grace's $

$2	$2	$2	$2	$2	$2	$2
$2	$2	$2	$2	$2	$2	$2	$2

15 X 2 = 30
Grace earned $30

Gabby's $

$3	$3	$3	$3	$3	$3
$3	$3	$3	$3	$3	$3

12 X 3 = 36
Gabby earned $36

30 + 36 = 66
Altogether, the cupcakes earned $66.

practice party

These great games turn math practice into math play!

MATH WAR

You will need two players and a deck of playing cards.

1. Remove face cards from the deck. Aces count as 1s.

2. Shuffle the cards and divide them into two equal stacks.

3. Give each player a stack with the cards facing down.

4. To play, players each flip over one card at the same time. The first player to shout the sum of the two card values collects the two cards and puts them on the bottom of her stack. In case of a tie, each player flips another card, and the first person to say the new sum wins all four cards.

5. The player who collects all of the cards is the winner.

WAR TIMES

Play with multiplication, too. When the cards are flipped, the first player to shout the product wins the cards.

HOP, SKIP, and JUMP

In this game, players practice skip-counting, or counting in blocks of a certain number value. To skip-count by 5s, for example, you say, "5, 10, 15, 20, 25, 30, 35," and so on. You will need four or more players.

1. Players sit in a circle.

2. One player starts by naming a number other than 1.

3. The player to her left skip-counts by the number the first player named, saying the next number. If the first player said 7, the next player says 14.

4. The next player to the left says the next number in the series, and so on.

5. If a player says the wrong number or takes more than 5 seconds for her turn, she gets a point. She then chooses a new number to start the next round.

6. When a player has 3 points, she is out. The last player in the game is the winner.

HIGH JUMP

To make the game more challenging, count by two- or three-digit numbers.

number namer

Play this game the same way you would play 20 Questions.
You need at least two players.

1. One player thinks of a whole number—any number.

2. Other players can ask up to 20 yes-or-no math questions to try to figure out what the number is.

3. The first person who says the number is the winner.

4. Let a different player choose a number and answer questions for each round.

Is it an odd number?

Is it higher than . . . ?

Is it divisible by 5?

Is it lower than . . . ?

Is it a prime number?

DICE DASH

You will need two or more players, a pencil and paper for each player, and three six-sided dice.

1. Before play begins, each player writes the numbers 1 through 10 on her paper.

2. The first player rolls the three dice together.

3. Using any two of the numbers rolled and any math operations, she finds combinations with solutions of 1 through 10, *in order*. For example, if she rolls . . .

She can make 1 by showing 3 - 2 = 1
She can make 2 by showing 5 - 3 = 2
She can make 3 by showing 5 - 2 = 3

She crosses the numbers 1, 2, and 3 off her list. She cannot make 4, so her turn ends, and the next player rolls. If the next player rolls . . .

. . . she cannot cross any numbers off her list, because no combination of math operations and the numbers she rolled makes 1. Her turn ends.

4. The first player to cross off all the numbers 1 through 10, in order, wins.

MENTAL MATH

Save time by doing math in your mind!

In math class, you use pencil and paper to help you solve problems. But when math comes up in everyday life, sometimes it's best to figure in your head. Follow these tips that take advantage of the Base 10 system to make mental math easier.

BREAK IT DOWN

Break down numbers by place value. Then complete single-digit math operations. Put the number back together when you're done to find your answer.

For an addition problem like

376 + 121 = ?

you might think

300 + 100 = 400 and
70 + 20 = 90 and
6 + 1 = 7

to come up with the answer:
497

For a multiplication problem like

243 × 7 = ?

you might think

200 × 7 = 1,400
40 × 7 = 280
3 × 7 = 21

and then

1,000 +
400 + 200 +
80 + 20 +
1 =

to come up with the answer:
1,701

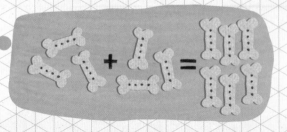

THINK IN TENS

Certain pairs of numbers add up to 10. Memorizing them helps when you want to add larger numbers or figure out addition problems in your head.

1 + 9 = 10

2 + 8 = 10

3 + 7 = 10

4 + 6 = 10

5 + 5 = 10

6 + 4 = 10

7 + 3 = 10

8 + 2 = 10

9 + 1 = 10

Group numbers so that they add up to 10 (or 100, or 1,000, and so on) to make quick work of adding.

In a problem like

162 + 47

you might look at the numbers in each place value and see if there are any pairs that equal 10. And yes! We see 162 + 47—with the 6 and 4 in the 10s place, which is the same as 60 plus 40, which equals 100.

So then you'd think of the sum as

100 + 100 + 2 + 7 = 209

from 162

from 60 + 40

from 162 and 47

For a problem like

3 + 8 + 7 + 5 + 2 + 5

you might look at the string, find the pairs of 10s, and think

3 + 7 = 10

8 + 2 = 10

5 + 5 = 10

10 + 10 + 10 = 30

USE GROUPS

Sometimes you already know how to count by a certain number. Use that skill to your advantage when you can. For example, you may feel comfortable counting by 25s if you think about counting quarters.

For a problem like
9 × 25

you might think

8 × 25 = 200 (just like 8 quarters = $2.00)
+ 25 (plus one more quarter) =
225

Here's another grouping trick: Multiplying by 5 is the same as multiplying by 10 and then dividing by 2. That's because

5 × 2 = 10
10 ÷ 5 = 2
and
10 ÷ 2 = 5

So for a problem like
2,133 × 5

you might think

2,133 × 10 = 21,330
21,330 ÷ 2 =
10,665

Give it a try! See if you can solve these problems without pencil and paper. Hint: Use Base 10.

4. $19 \times 25 =$?

1. $57 + 552 =$?

5. $277 - 113 =$?

2. $1{,}234 + 9{,}876 =$?

6. $1{,}084 - 973 =$?

3. $223 \times 3 =$?

7. $98 \times 5 =$?

(answers on page 93)

Terrific Tests

These hints will help you do your best on math tests.

STUDY SMART

What's the #1 way to study for a math test? Practice! Choose sample problems from the chapters or units your test will cover and do them—even if you've already completed the problems in class or as homework.

Cramming for exams does not work as well as studying in short bursts for a week or so before your test. So spread out your study sessions! Review your assignments and class notes several days before the test. If you see any topics or kinds of problems you don't understand, ask your teacher for help before the test. Practice problems throughout the week. Do one last review the night before the test to make sure you're ready.

THINGS TO DO!

Be the teacher! One great way to see if you understand something is to teach it to someone else. Teach the math methods you're studying to a friend, sibling, or parent.

TEST TIME

Read the directions! You can't get problems right if you don't know what you're supposed to do. Always read all test directions carefully before you begin work.

Do the problems you know first. Come back to more challenging problems after you complete all the problems you're comfortable with.

Show all your work. Sometimes teachers give partial credit if you use the correct method to solve a problem but get an incorrect answer because of a simple error.

Use the test as a resource. Sometimes you can find hints for problems you can't answer elsewhere on your test. Maybe the formula you need appears in another problem. Maybe the term you forgot is defined in another question.

Check your work! If you finish your test before time is up, double-check your answers before you turn it in.

FEELING SOME NERVES?

Come prepared. Study throughout the week before your test. Bring all the materials you need. And get to class early.

Right before your test begins, take a few minutes to write down all your test worries. Studies show this exercise can ease nervous feelings and improve test scores!

If you feel panicked during a test, take a few deep breaths. Then do the problems you know. When you're done, see if the rest of the test looks less scary.

Remember, everyone is made for math. Your mind does calculations all day, every day. Everyone can do it! Everyone is a "math person." You, too!

WHAT'S YOUR MATH MIGHT?

Which statements apply to you?
Find your strength and make the most of it!

When I eat at a restaurant, I usually figure out the correct tip before my parents do.

I could easily use a scaled map to figure out about how far one city is from another.

I'm great at timed tests in math class. Bring on the math facts!

I love shopping at sales. It's no problem for me to figure out discounted prices when a sign says 25% off—or more!

I'm best at math that calls for me to show my work.

Geometry is fun for me. Shapes bring math ideas to life.

I'm good at math that I do in my head, without a pencil and paper.

I'm best at math that lets me look at and compare shapes, sizes, or pictures.

If I have pencil and paper, I can figure out just about any basic math problem.

In a grocery store, I can figure out which size product is the best deal.

I prefer math problems with just numbers. Story problems and charts are not my favorite.

I like to draw pictures or diagrams or use graph paper to solve tricky problems.

answers

Did you choose mostly **purples?** You have a talent for mental math! Plus, you're good at applying your skill to the math you face in your everyday life. In math class, you might find you know the answers before other students do. Be sure to show your work, though, when you're supposed to. Sometimes the teacher needs to see your thought process to check that you understand new concepts.

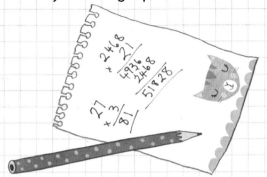

Did you select **reds** the most? You're clever at computation! Math homework and tests don't faze you. And you always show your work. Don't be afraid to move math away from your comfort zone of pencil on paper. Your talent will transfer outside the classroom.

Did you go for mostly **greens?** You're skilled at visualizing math problems, and thinking of concrete objects helps you find the answers. You're great at seeing math relationships in the shapes around you. As long as you keep sharp on your basic math facts, you can use pictures, diagrams, and shapes to solve most math problems.

BIG IDea!

Here's the thing: We all think about math in different ways. There's not a right way versus a wrong way to solve a math problem. Mental math, computation, and visualization are all great methods for finding solutions! Make the most of your strength. But when you get stuck, give another method a try. Use your mathematical mind!

math in real life

Put your number knowledge to use every day!

money MaTH

There's clear value in mastering the math of money.

savinG money

The equation for saving is simple:
money × time = savings

If you want to figure out how long it will take you to save a certain amount of money, just follow two simple steps:

1. Decide how much money you can save every week.

2. Divide the total amount of money you want to save by the weekly amount you decided you can save. The solution to this division problem will tell you how many weeks it will take you to reach your goal.

For instance, say you want to buy a tablet that costs $160. Every week, you earn $6 allowance and $10 for babysitting. That's $16. Now do the math:

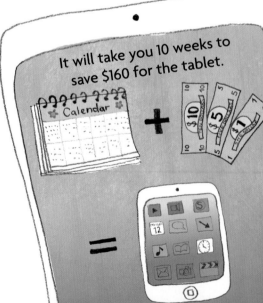

It will take you 10 weeks to save $160 for the tablet.

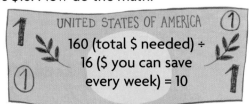

UNITED STATES OF AMERICA
160 (total $ needed) ÷
16 ($ you can save
every week) = 10

Sale Prices

Surprise! When your dad takes you to the mall to buy the tablet, you find out it's on sale. The sign at the store says:

To figure out the sale price, you first need to calculate the **sale percent.** That's the amount you get to subtract from the original price.

How do you calculate 25% of $160, the original price of the tablet? You can use a couple of methods:

Method 1

Think of the percent as a fraction: 25% is the same as 25/100, which is the same as ¼. What's ¼ of $160? With mental math, you can figure it's $40.

Method 2

Think of the percent as a decimal number: 25% is the same as .25.

So the question "25% of $160 is how much?" can be written mathematically as ".25 × 160 = ?" because the word "of" tells you to multiply.

When you solve that equation on paper, it's easier to put the larger number on top. The answer is the same. Just be sure to add the decimal point to your product.

$$
\begin{array}{r}
\$1\,6\,0 \\
\times\ .2\,5 \\
\hline
8\,0\,0 \\
+\,3\,2\,0 \\
\hline
\$4\,0.\,0\,0
\end{array}
$$

Whether you figure it in your head or on paper, you know the sale percent is $40. Now subtract the sale percent from the original price to find the sale price:

$$\$160 - \$40 = ?$$

The sale price for the tablet is $120.

sales tax

But wait! You're still not done. You might need to pay **sales tax** in addition to the price. Imagine that the sales tax on the tablet is 5%. How much money will you need in total? To get that number, figure out the amount of the tax, and then add it to the sale price.

5% is the same as .05. Also, 5% is half of 10% (or .10, or simply .1).

Percent means "out of 100," just like a dollar is based on 100 pennies. So 5% would be like 5 pennies, or .05.

$$.1 \times 120 = 12$$
$$\text{Half of } 12 = 6$$

So $6 is the sales tax amount you'll add to the purchase price of the tablet.

$$\$120 + \$6 = ?$$

You will need $126 to buy that tablet.

managing your money

Keep records of the money you earn, save, and spend. Use a notebook, a ledger book, or a computer. Recording how you use money lets you see clearly where your money goes and how it grows. You'll create great habits for the future, and you'll get some math practice, too!

EARN

Walk Mrs. J's $37
(April) dog

SPEND

Movie $8

Mom's Birthday $12
Present

Ice Cream with $3
Eva

DO YOU KNOW THE SCORE?

Get out a sheet of scratch paper and challenge yourself to see how math is a key player in the world of sports.

1. If Leanne threw two 6-point touchdowns and Bri kicked five 3-point field goals, who scored more points?

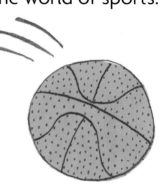

2. There's one minute left in the basketball championship game, and Fiona's team is down by 12 points. How many regular baskets at 2 points each does her team need to tie the score?

3. Mia ran 400 meters in 90 seconds, and Shelina ran a kilometer in 4 minutes. Which girl ran her race at a faster pace?

4. If Jillian got 6 hits in 18 times at bat, and Rochelle got 13 hits in 30 times at bat, who has the better batting average?

5. Sixteen teams will compete in Hallie's volleyball tournament. Each team plays one match per round. The winner of each match moves on to the next round until only the champion remains. How many matches will Hallie's team play if they win the tournament?

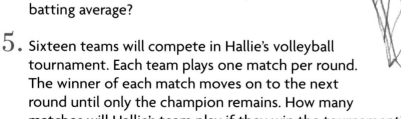

(answers on page 93)

ABOUT TIME

It's tricky to calculate on the clock!

If you go to school from 8:00 in the morning until 3:00 in the afternoon, how many hours does your school day last?

To get an answer, you might count the hours on the clock: 8, 9, 10, 11, 12, 1, 2, 3. And you'd guess 8 hours. But that's not correct. Your school day actually lasts 7 hours.

When you count hours, 1 is the full hour that begins at 8:00 and ends at 9:00, 2 is the hour between 9:00 and 10:00, and so on. If you count the hours on the clock face in this way, as the space between the numbers, you'll count to 7. Here's another way to look at it: Because the first hour ends at 9:00, start counting at 9:00 rather than 8:00.

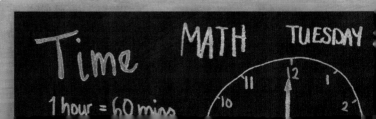

TIMε IT RIGHT

1. You have an important math exam tomorrow, and you want to make sure you get at least 10 hours of shut-eye before the big test. You need to wake up at 6:45 a.m. When do you need to be asleep?

2. Your mom says you and your older sister can go to the movies and the arcade this afternoon while she runs errands. Your movie starts at 2:45 p.m. and it lasts 1 hour and 45 minutes. Then you can go to the arcade for another hour and a half. When will your mom pick you up?

3. You love to bake bread in your family's bread machine. The machine has a timer that lets you put the ingredients in the machine but delay when it starts baking. You want your loaf finished at 6:00 p.m., in time for dinner. The machine's bake cycle lasts 4 hours. How long should you delay the start of the bake cycle if you set the timer at 7:30 a.m., before you leave for school?

(answers on page 94)

MMMMaTH!

Get cooking with some recipe math.

Did you know that great cooks need great math skills? Successful chefs must measure accurately. They also need to be able to divide or multiply to make smaller or larger quantities of a recipe. Let's say you want to make lasagna from a recipe that says "Feeds eight hungry people." But you're feeding only four. You'll need to **convert,** or change, all of the ingredient amounts.

Sometimes cooking conversions aren't as simple or easy as changing a whole cup to a half cup. So it helps to have a conversion chart.

Conversions for Cooks

THIS	is the same as	THIS
1 tablespoon (1 T, 1 tbsp)	----->	3 teaspoons (3 t, 3 tsp)
¼ cup (¼ c)	----->	4 tablespoons
1 cup	----->	16 tablespoons
1 cup	----->	8 fluid ounces (8 fl oz)
1 pint (1 pt)	----->	2 cups
1 quart (1 qt)	----->	2 pints
1 gallon (1 gal)	----->	4 quarts
1 gallon	----->	16 cups
1 pound (1 lb)	----->	16 ounces (16 oz)

COOKING CONVERSIONS

Use the chart to practice making changes.

1. You're baking half a batch of cookies. The full-size recipe calls for ¼ cup of raisins and 3 cups of oats. How much of each should you measure out?

2. Your applesauce recipe calls for 2 teaspoons of cinnamon. You just went apple picking, so you're making a triple batch. How many tablespoons of cinnamon do you need?

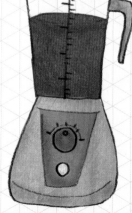

3. Your recipe for one smoothie calls for ½ cup of blueberries. You find a whole pint of blueberries in the fridge. How many smoothies can you make?

(answers on page 94)

COOKING CHALLENGE!

Find your favorite recipe to make with your mom or dad. Make a list of the ingredients, and figure the amounts needed if you cut the recipe in half. Then list the amounts you'd need to make a double batch.

CHEF'S NOTE

When you make a big batch of a recipe or cut it down, cooking times don't change the way ingredient amounts do. A double-size cake won't take twice as long to bake. You'll need to monitor cooking closely to get the timing right.

Grocery Games

Skillful shoppers convert, calculate, and compare prices. Can you spot the better bargain in each pair of products? Use the conversion chart on page 80 for help.

1.
a. ICE-CREAM RICH & CREAMY FUDGEY 1 PINT
ICE-CREAM RICH & CREAMY CHOCOLATE SWIRL 1 PINT
ICE-CREAM RICH & CREAMY BERRYLICIOUS
3 FOR $6

b. ALL NATURAL HALF GALLON ICE-CREAM CHOC-CHIP COOKIE DOUGH
$6

2.
a. YUMMY PEANUT BUTTER N°1 1 POUND
$3.20

b. YUMMY PEANUT BUTTER N°1 40 OUNCES
$6.40

3.
a. ORANGE JUICE ½ GALLON
$4.95

b. ORANGE JUICE 8 OZ (×6)
$4.95

4.
a. APPLES 1 POUND
$2.50

b. apple slices SUPER JUICY! 4 oz
3 BAGS $1 each!

5.
a. BERRY MUFFINS 1 DOZEN
$3

b. 50¢ EACH

(answers on page 94)

MORE MAGIC MATH

Entertain yourself and your friends
with more math tricks and puzzles.

DIVINE NINE

Try this trick on a friend. She may want scratch
paper or a calculator, so have it handy.

Now I'll amaze you once more!

1. Ask your friend to pick a number,
any number, 10 or higher.

2. Tell her to add the digits of the
number together.

3. Next, have her subtract that sum
from her original number.

4. Tell her you can predict the future.
Say, "I know the number you have
now is divisible by 9." Have her divide
the number by 9. The new number
should be a whole number, and
she'll say, "Wow! You're right!"

5. Say, "Now I'll amaze you once more!
Add the digits of your new number
together. The total will be 9 or a
multiple of 9!"

This math magic will work no matter what number your friend chooses.
For example, say your friend selects 941. Here's what the trick would look like:

(STEP 2) 9 + 4 + 1 = 14

(STEP 3) 941 – 14 = 927

(STEP 4) 927 ÷ 9 = 103 (no remainder!)

(STEP 5) 9 + 2 + 7 = 18 (multiple of 9!)

SIMPLE SUDOKU

Fill in the grids below. Each row, column, and colored box of four squares should contain the numbers 1 through 4 without repeating a number in any row, column, or colored box.

(answers on page 94)

super series

Puzzle a group of pals with some fast math! Give everyone paper and pencil and ask one friend to suggest a number between 1 and 100. Then say you'll race the group to see who can add up all the numbers from 1 to that number in the fastest time. Use this trick and be the one to find the sum first.

1. Multiply the number your friend suggested by 1 less than that number.

2. Divide that product by 2.

3. Add the original number . . .

. . . and that's your answer! While your friends are adding 1 + 2 + 3 + 4 . . . , you've found the solution in three easy steps.

Here's an example:

Suppose your friend chooses the number 15.

Multiply 15 by the number that's 1 less: 15 × 14 = 210

Divide the product by 2: 210 ÷ 2 = 105

Add the original number: 105 + 15 = 120

The total for the numbers from 1 to 15 is 120. Want proof? Check the math using scratch paper or a calculator.

Number (22)
. 22 × 21 = 4
. 462 ÷ 2 = 23
231 + 22 = 253
Answer = 253

MATH MESSAGES

Match numbers and letters to send your friends secret notes! Assign a number value to each letter of the alphabet. It's simple to begin with A = 1, B = 2, C = 3, and so on, all the way to Z = 26. Use your code to write messages like this:

8 9, 6 18 9 5 14 4!

To complicate your code, just shift your starting value. For example, you might say that A = 20, B = 21, C = 22, and so on. When you get to 26, just wrap around and start at 1 again.

So, if A = 20, then G = 26 and H = 1.

Pass a coded note to a friend and tell her the value for A. She'll be able to decode the message, but the code will be hard to crack for anyone else.

Hi, friend!

Are Numbers In Your Future?

Many cool careers involve math skills. Which of these statements sound like you? Choose as many as you like—then turn the page to see how you might use math in the future.

I love to experiment with computers.

I'm interested in business and the stock market.

I like to make things. Want a birdhouse built — or a sweater knit? I'm your girl.

I like teaching my friends how to do new things.

I'm great at keeping track of the money I earn and spend.

I like figuring out how machines work.

I'm interested in architecture or design—I like thinking about how shapes and lines fit together.

I'm really good at explaining things.

I'm fascinated by the stars, planets, and travel in space.

I enjoy following the stats for my favorite sports team.

I'm into drawing, painting, or taking photos.

When my friends or siblings need help with homework, they often ask me.

I like to create in the kitchen.

I love to be outside. I'm a nature buff.

I'm full of big ideas for new projects or products. I can't wait to make them happen!

I consider myself a people person.

answers

If you picked any **red** answers, you might see yourself pursuing a science career. Computer programmers, engineers, doctors, and scientists of all kinds use math every day! Math is their key tool for figuring out how things work and showing precisely how their ideas fit together.

If you chose any **blues,** perhaps you can imagine yourself in teaching. Math teachers aren't the only educators whose work is math-minded. Teachers of all subjects working with all levels of students use math to explain ideas, set schedules, assign grades, and more.

If you selected any **green** answers, maybe you're thinking about a creative career. The fact is, you need math to make just about anything. In visual arts and design, for example, math helps you express relationships between sizes and shapes. And when you're crafting or cooking, your success depends upon measuring and proportion.

If you picked any **purples,** you might imagine yourself in business. It's easy to see math at work in business careers such as accountant, banker, or stockbroker. But every businessperson needs math to keep track of finances, orders, production, scheduling, and much more!

ONE THING IS FOR CERTAIN: WHATEVER CAREER YOU CHOOSE, MATH WILL BE PART OF IT!

So engage your mind
and make the most of math class.

Keep practicing, and ask for help when you need it.

CELEBRATE YOUR SUCCESSES.

And embrace the
"math person" inside you!

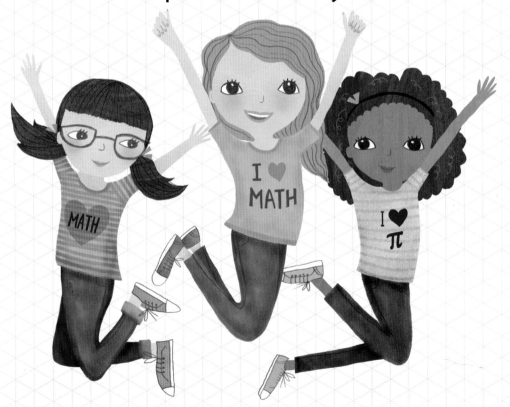

answers

Page 37: Criss-Cross Math

The criss-cross grid contains:

Row 1: 6 8 | 6 8 | | | | 4
Row: 7 | 4 2 | 2 4
Row: 9 8 7 | | 4 | 1
Row: 0 | 6 0 0 0 | 0
Row: 5 0 0 | 1 | 1 | 8 | 1
Row: 4 | 2 0 0 0 0 | 0
Row: 3 | 3 | 2 | 1
Row: 4 | 9 | 8 | 0
Row: 5 5 | 1 0 1

Page 38: Sum Search

40	30	20	10	17	16	4
5	9	42	80	9	33	5
50	12	39	10	33	14	18
5	50	99	33	21	18	19
88	24	1	94	19	25	5
33	35	38	20	19	25	1
54	29	21	44	21	25	7
14	22	10	15	20	25	30

92

Page 49: Math Maze

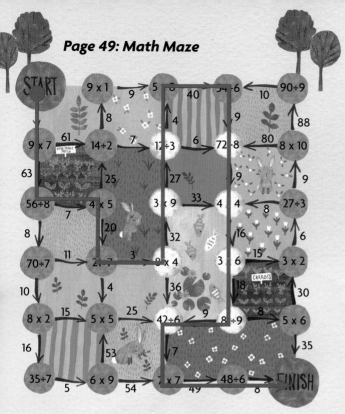

Page 67: Mental Math

1. 609

2. 11,110

3. 669

4. 475

5. 164

6. 111

7. 490

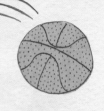

Page 77: Do You Know the Score?

1. Bri scored more points. Her 5 field goals at 3 points apiece scored a total of 15 (5 × 3 = 15), while Leanne's 2 touchdowns at 6 points apiece scored 12 (2 × 6 = 12).

2. If regular baskets earn 2 points, Fiona's team needs to shoot 6 baskets to tie the score. Bonus: If they have one minute, or 60 seconds, to do it, they need to shoot a basket every 10 seconds!

3. When you do the math in the same terms, you see that Mia ran faster. Her pace was about 4.44 meters per second: 400 meters ÷ 90 seconds = 4.444 meters/second. Shelina ran about 4.17 meters per second: 1 kilometer = 1,000 meters and 4 minutes = 240 seconds; 1,000 meters ÷ 240 seconds = 4.166 meters/second.

4. You can write Jillian's average as 6/18, which is the same as 6 ÷ 18, which equals about .333. Rochelle has the higher average—about .433.

5. Hallie's team will play 4 matches: 1 when all 16 teams play, 1 when 8 teams remain, 1 when 4 teams remain, and the final match between the last 2 teams.

Page 79: About Time

1. Counting back 10 hours from 6:45 a.m., you know you need to be sleeping by 8:45 the night before.

2. Your mom will pick you up at 6:00.

3. If it takes 4 hours for the bread to bake and you want it ready at 6:00 p.m., you want to start the machine baking at 2:00 p.m. The time between 7:30 a.m. and 2:00 in the afternoon is 6 hours, 30 minutes, the amount of time you need to delay the bake cycle.

Page 81: Cooking Conversions

1. You need 2 tablespoons of raisins and 1½ cups of oats.

2. You need 2 tablespoons of cinnamon.

3. You can make 4 smoothies.

Page 83: Grocery Games

1. b
2. b
3. a
4. a
5. a

Page 86: Simple Sudoku

1	3	4	2		3	2	4	1
2	4	1	3		1	4	2	3
3	1	2	4		4	3	1	2
4	2	3	1		2	1	3	4
4	2	3	1		2	4	1	3
3	1	2	4		1	3	2	4
1	3	4	2		3	1	4	2
2	4	1	3		4	2	3	1

MaTH GLossary

Altogether: indicates an addition problem

Ballpark estimate: rounding numbers up or down to help you guess what your solution will be close to

Convert: to change from one term to another, as in: 1 foot converts to 12 inches, or 1 quart converts to 4 cups

Difference: the answer or solution to a subtraction problem

Dividend: the number that you separate or divide

Divisor: the number of groups that you separate a dividend into

Fact families: related addition/subtraction or multiplication/division facts made from the same numbers

Factors: numbers that you multiply together

Greater than: a relationship indicated by the symbol >

Inverse: opposite

Less than: a relationship indicated by the symbol <

Manipulatives: objects used to help you solve math problems

Prime number: a number that is divisible only by 1 and itself (but not including the number 1)

Product: the answer or solution to a multiplication problem

Quotient: the answer or solution to a division problem

Remainder: the amount left over when a number isn't evenly divisible

Solution: the answer to a math problem

Square number: a number that is the product of the same two numbers, such as 9, which is the product of 3 multiplied by itself

Sum: the answer or solution to an addition problem

Do you have a math tip or triumph to share?

Write to us!
School RULES! Math Editor
American Girl
8400 Fairway Place
Middleton, WI 53562

Here are some other American Girl® books you might like.

Each sold separately. Find more books online at americangirl.com.

Discover online games, quizzes, activities,
and more at **americangirl.com/play**